ITALIAN

✦ FOLK MAGIC ✦

Publisher
Balthazar Pagani

Graphic design and layout
Bebung

Editing and fact checking Giulia Bilancetti

Vivida

Vivida® is a registered trademark property of White Star s.r.l.

© 2026 White Star s.r.l.
Piazzale Luigi Cadorna, 6
20123 Milan, Italy
www.whitestar.it

Translation: Iceigeo, Milano (Alexa Ahern)
Editing: Abby Young

ISBN 978-88-544-2185-1
1 2 3 4 5 6   30 29 28 27 26

Printed in China

(+)

Azzurra D'Agostino

ITALIAN

+ FOLK MAGIC +

ILLUSTRATIONS BY
Elisa Macellari

(+)

Vivida

CONTENTS

(✦)

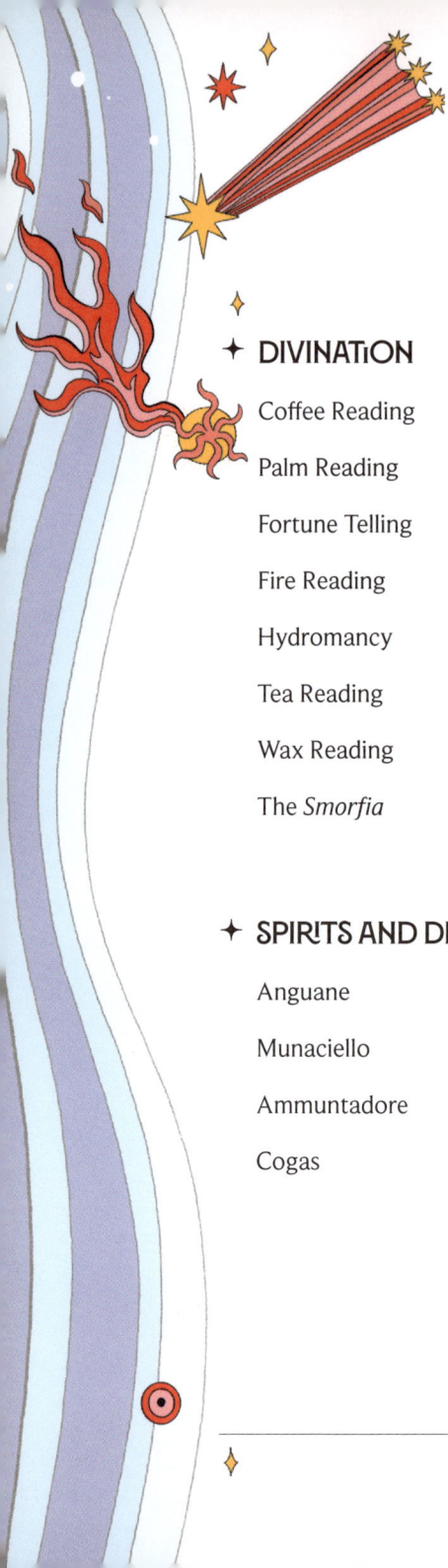

✦ HISTORICAL FIGURES   108

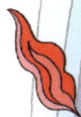

INTRODUCTION

(+)

I taly is unique for its diversity from region to region, which is evident in the different accents, dialects, cuisines, and traditions. And, of course, also in the beliefs, legends, and rituals. Throughout the country there is a penchant for superstitious gestures — from throwing a pinch of salt over your shoulder to touching a doorpost and making the sign of the horns with your fingers.

ONE COMMON ELEMENT TO ALMOST ANY MAGICAL PRACTICE IN ITALY, FROM NORTH TO SOUTH, IS A SHARED BELIEF IN SUPERSTITION.

One of the most striking examples is perhaps the *Smorfia*, of Neapolitan origin. It is a book that translates dreams into numbers to play in the lottery, and every week millions of

people try their luck this way. Each number in the book, which is used throughout Italy, represents a dream image, such as "women's legs," which corresponds to 77. The significance of these combinations of numbers is also demonstrated by the fact that when playing bingo, some numbers are today still called by the name of the associated image, such as "dead man speaking" instead of "48."

WHILE THERE ARE A FEW SUPERSTITIOUS GESTURES COMMON THROUGHOUT THE PENINSULA, SOME THINGS ARE STRICTLY REGIONAL.

Magical figures, spirits, and gods vary considerably from one area to another, often linked to ancient pagan traditions that had very different origins. In the North, for example, there are Celtic influences, while in Sardinia there are customs from pre-Roman cultures. Spells and magical rituals are in some cases intertwined with food, one of the most deeply rooted aspects of Italian culture. It is not uncommon for potions and rituals to be prepared with ingredients typical of Mediterranean cuisine, first and foremost olive oil. A hypothetical "witch's cave" in Italy cannot be separated from the image of a garden full of plants and the fragrances of local fruits and spices.

Even many of the figures present throughout the peninsula, despite their different names and appearances, share common characteristics. It is interesting to note that many of these are impersonal, that is, they represent a category (for example, a type of healer) rather than a specific person.

IT IS A ROLE THAT IS HANDED DOWN FROM GENERATION TO GENERATION, AND ALTHOUGH IT EXISTED (AND OFTEN STILL EXISTS), IT CANNOT BE IDENTIFIED WITH A SINGLE HISTORICALLY PLACED PROTAGONIST.

However, they have many characteristics in common: they can heal, they are associated with rituals that involve formulas and the use of plants or symbolic elements (from olive branches to silver coins), they cannot be paid for their services, and they are often elderly people who have inherited their powers from a family member.

It is evident how all these elements are closely intertwined and sustain a culture that, even in today's reified world, continues to preserve in its secret substratum magical elements, small superstitious rituals, and a certain link to the legends and gifts of the natural world and the landscape. Although slowly fading with the passing of generations, it profoundly shapes the identity of this people.

MAGIC, SPELLS, AND MAGICAL PRACTICES

The large number of healers and curers present in popular traditions throughout Italy is linked to the existence of a wide range of magical practices, some of which survive to this day. Many are associated with healing rites, which often combine folk medicine with remedies that testify to a deep knowledge of medicinal plants. These spells are designed to ward off various types of ailments, both physical, such as pimples or whooping cough, and subtle, related to enchantments and affecting the emotional-spiritual realm. These could be the evil eye, fear, or any of a number of psycho-physical symptoms related to what are now clinically defined as depression or anxiety. Magical practices are used not only to ward off evil but also to protect and promote good. For example, there are rituals for good luck, love potions, formulas that guarantee economic prosperity, and the successful outcome of exams. In Italy, there are also deeply rooted superstitious gestures that don't require an intermediary. For example, the custom of rubbing behind the ears with fingers dipped in a drop of spilled wine, an apotropaic gesture believed to bring abundance and good fortune.

(✦)

WARDING OFF THE EVIL EYE

The evil eye is a gaze that derives from evil or envious thoughts, negative energy, and black magic. It is believed that it can harm those who are afflicted by it, causing a wide range of symptoms, from physical problems such as headaches or weakness to mental problems such as unjustified fears or mistrust of others, as well as educational, financial, or family difficulties. More broadly, it is often associated with general bad luck. There are many ways to prevent it. In Sardinia, a pendant called *su coccu* made of black obsidian, onyx, or opal is used as an amulet; elsewhere, black agate, rock salt, black tourmaline, and tiger's eye are used. In the Marche and several other regions, a red bow or ribbon is pinned to children's clothing to protect them. In the Neapolitan area, a nursery rhyme is recited and the gesture of the horns or the sign of the cross is made. When infected, a healer is needed to remove the curse. Often this is an elderly woman who speaks the secret words after pouring oil into water, symbolically cutting it with scissors, and throwing it in a place where it will never be stepped on.

(+)

CURING SHINGLES

T oday we know that this painful rash is caused by herpes zoster, the same virus that causes chickenpox. In Italian, it is called *fuoco di Sant'Antonio*, after Saint Anthony Abate, both because of his association with fire (it is said that he stole a spark from the underworld to give it to humanity) and because of the miracular powers attributed to him, especially for curing this disease. The ritual, which is still practiced in Italy today, requires the presence of a specific person called a *segnatore* or *segnatrice* (sign maker). People with this power make *segnatura*, or symbolic signs traced with the hands around the infected blisters; these gestures are accompanied by secret powerful words. Sometimes the *segnatura* is done with a piece of warm charcoal, drawing circles around the diseased area a certain number of times, ending with a cross and a secret formula of protection and invocation of healing. The ritual must be repeated three times on different days. In the Tuscan-Emilian Apennines, blackberry leaves are used instead of charcoal.

(+)

CURING SCABIES

Scabies is a skin irritation caused by mites that makes the areas between the fingers and toes and the groin extremely itchy. It is now mainly treated with ointments and anti-infectives. In the past, this disease was very common, and the traditional remedies were phytotherapy or sulfur-based compresses. These were, and in some cases still are, accompanied by magical rituals to cure it. In Abruzzo, for example, there is a small church in the middle of the woods dedicated to St. John. There is a spring with the same name where people suffering from scabies go on the night of the saint's feast day (between June 23 and 24) to ritually wash themselves with the water, which is believed to have miraculous properties. Among the popular remedies is the preparation of a pink ointment obtained by passing butter through rose water several times. Ligurian tradition attributes magical properties to rose syrup or jam, which can combat epidemics and plagues, including scabies.

(+)

CURING JAUNDICE

Over the centuries, there have been many magical rituals thought to cure jaundice, a liver disease that causes the skin and whites of the eyes to turn yellow. In Magna Graecia (southern Italy), it was believed that if you stared hard at a bird like a plover and it returned your gaze, you would be cured of the disease. A 16th-century recipe called for picking a cabbage plant that had never been transplanted, cooking it for three consecutive mornings, and feeding it to the patient without any seasoning. In Tuscany and central Italy, saffron was used instead: the healer, endowed with special powers, had to "mark" the patient, accompanying the gestures with secret magical formulas. In Basilicata, jaundice was called "the disease of the arch" and it was said that it could be cured by urinating in the direction of a rainbow. The patient had to get up before dawn, not speak to anyone, and pass under three brick arches while reciting a ritual formula. In this way, the disease he had absorbed from the rainbow would return to the stone arches.

(+)

CURING SUNSTROKE

In Sicily, sunstroke was common among farmers working in the fields. There were two magic rituals believed to "remove the sun." To perform the first, the person is made to sit indoors, with doors and windows that do not let in light, and the ritual is performed three times, morning and evening, on an empty stomach. The person performing the ritual quickly holds a half-full glass of water over the patient's forehead. While the healer recites some formulas, bubbles form in the water. When these stop, the sunstroke is considered cured. The other rite takes place at sunset: a red cloth, a plate with a little water, and a wick made of cotton and oil are placed on the patient's head; then a glass is overturned on the wick, which burns and consumes the oxygen, causing the water to be sucked up by the cotton. This should be repeated three times and for a varying number of days (at least three, or seven, or nine) until the water is no longer sucked up. A variant of this practice, with a coin and a different formula, is also widespread in Liguria.

(+)

CURING
A STYE

A stye is an inflammation of the eye that causes swelling and redness of the eyelid, where a rather painful yellow "spot" forms. It is of infectious origin and today there are various treatments to cure it, but in Italy it has always been associated with magical or semi-magical rituals that are considered capable of eliminating it. Since it was believed to be caused by the curse of a pregnant woman who was offered food she didn't like, people usually turned to healers (almost always women) who could "mark" it. These healers would make the sign of the cross over the eye several times with a silver ring or rosary beads. In Florence, on the other hand, it was said to "go and have your eye sewn," because here the ritual required the healer to simulate the act of sewing the eye with a needle and thread while uttering magic words. Another way to cure it, according to popular belief, was to make the person look at the bottom of a bottle of olive oil, with the affected eye resting on its opening.

(+)

LOVE SPELLS

There are many rituals and magical practices related to love. Throughout Italy and throughout history, magic has been used to help with matters of the heart. They were often carried out by specific characters, experts in spells and potions (see the chapter "Historical Figures"). In Apulia, as in other regions, the symbolism of knots and ties was used to emphasize the bond of love. For example, a rejected suitor might place a small braid of wool under his beloved's mattress to bind their destinies together; a woman who wanted to attract a certain suitor might tie a ribbon three times while repeating a magic formula, a superstitious ritual to be performed only in odd months. In Sicily, there was the *legamento col caffè*, or "binding with coffee": coffee was prepared according to a specific procedure and given to the person who was suffering from love or to the person one wanted to bind, using a candle during the ritual to which ground coffee was added to the wax.

(+)

LUCK SPELLS

Luck spells are in some cases actions that defend against evil spells and the evil eye, thus they are protective and favor good luck. In Salento (Apulia) there was a custom, in some cases still observed, of hanging scissors next to the front door, on walls or balconies, to prevent gossips from harming the family, symbolically "cutting them" before they enter. Throughout rural Italy, even today, St. John's water is prepared on the night between June 23 and 24 to bring health and good luck. In the past, young women were invited to bathe in the dew-filled fields to promote fertility. Around the same time in June, with the summer solstice, symbols of fire were used in rituals to protect and bring health. Traditionally, nine herbs are burned: St. John's wort, lavender, rue, verbena, mugwort, lamb's tongue, fennel, thyme, and mistletoe to propitiate luck and abundance. In Veneto, until a few decades ago, fires were lit at crossroads, just as in ancient times large bonfires were lit on the night before the solstice, around which people would dance and sing.

(✦)

THE USE OF SALT

Salt has always been a valuable ingredient for humans to preserve food and add flavor. In popular belief, these beneficial properties have led to its use in superstitious practices and rituals. First, it was believed to keep away evil spirits, so sprinkling salt in the corners of the house was an effective way to protect it from the evil eye. It is also said to protect against envy by keeping three grains of salt in your wallet, and to bring good luck by throwing a handful of salt over your shoulder (in Italy, spilling salt at the table brings bad luck, and to reverse this ominous gesture, a pinch of the fallen salt is thrown behind one's shoulder). Another superstitious gesture is to never give or receive salt directly from another person. You should always put the salt shaker on the table first. This precaution is linked to the symbolic and material value of salt, so precious that it gave rise to the term "salary." Passing it from one hand to another could lead to a loss of money or to debt. Giving salt as a gift, on the other hand, is a sign of great fortune and prosperity.

(✦)

TOUCHING IRON

I n Italy, and in general in the Mediterranean region, there is the expression *toccare ferro*, or "touch iron," which is superstitious even when spoken. Usually, to wish good luck, the sign of the horns is made with the fingers, and they are used to touch an iron object. This ancient custom also gave us the simple gesture of the horns to indicate hope, good luck, or protection against an omen. The gesture is sometimes made when a coffin passes by or during a conversation in which one wishes to avoid a problem or hopes for a good outcome (such as a school or medical exam). "Touch iron" is an abbreviation of "touch a horseshoe" (*ferro di cavallo*), an object believed since the Middle Ages to protect the house from evil spirits and the evil eye. In fact, it was traditional to hang one on the door with an odd number of nails (with the open part facing up). Iron is also associated with weapons, a symbol of defense.

(✦)

THE BLACK CAT

Between the end of the Middle Ages and the beginning of the Modern Age, the superstition that black cats were bad omens began to spread, first in the Mediterranean region and later throughout the Western world. Fear of the animal became widespread during the witch hunts, when it was believed that the animal could have been a witch's accomplice or even a witch in a cat's body. The black cat was also mentioned in the papal bull of Pope Gregory IX, giving rise to the myth that it contained an order to exterminate all cats of that color. It is likely that the superstition stems from the symbolism of black as a color associated with death and mourning. The origin of the rumor that a black cat crossing our path brings bad luck (to the point that some people in Italy change the direction of their route) dates back to the time when people rode horses, since a cat, if it appeared suddenly, could scare the horse and cause the rider to fall. In 16th-century Italy, it was also believed that if a black cat were to lie down on a sick person's bed, death was imminent.

(+)

PLANTS AND PREPARATIONS

(+)

Italy is an abundant country, rich in fruits, wild herbs, and plants cultivated with wisdom from north to south. This natural wealth has traditionally favored a delicious, varied, and healthy cuisine, enriched by the traditional knowledge of the properties and uses of this range of products. This goes hand in hand with the ancient knowledge of the land and its fruits, which have always been used for healing and magic, as well as for food. The simplest and most humble plants have been used in preparations for magical rituals, such as to dispel fear, while others have been used to heal the body through the beneficial properties of local flowers, roots, and fruits. Ointments, herbal teas, magic potions, and recipes are part of the traditional Italian culture, which for centuries has skillfully blended its ingredients from culture and knowledge of the landscape and its gifts.

(+)

GARLIC

G arlic has been considered a magical plant for thousands of years. In the Middle Ages, it was believed to protect against the devil, as well as the plague and cholera. Its antiseptic properties are still recognized today, so much so that it is used in numerous natural preparations as an antioxidant and to keep cholesterol and blood pressure under control. The fact that it grows underground has always associated it with the occult. It is used as a defense against evil spirits (hence the belief that it keeps vampires away). This proximity to the underground world makes it a powerful amulet, often associated with abundance in many Italian traditions. In Emilia-Romagna, for example, there is a deep-rooted custom of buying a braid of garlic to ward off poverty for the rest of the year. In southern Italy, a clove of garlic is worn on June 22, the day before the eve of St. John's Day: this simple expedient keeps evil spirits away and prevents spells from working on the wearer.

(✦)

CHILI PEPPER

Widely used in traditional Italian cuisine, from Calabrian *soppressata* (a very spicy salami) to *penne all'arrabbiata* (a typical Roman pasta dish), chili peppers are not only rich in flavor but also have many symbolic properties. In Italy, the red horn-shaped amulet that you hang on your keychain or car mirror is a good luck charm that protects and brings good fortune. In Abruzzo, farmers used to hang a chili pepper braid behind their front door to ward off the evil eye and evil spirits. It is also a symbol of passionate love, energy, and strength, not only in the sexual sense. The whole plant can be used as a symbol of love and fidelity, while the single fruit is a good omen for success during an important event. It has anti-inflammatory properties, aids digestion, improves blood circulation, and is known to have a positive effect on mood. It also relieves muscle tension, which is why it is found as an ingredient in many pain-relieving balms.

(✦)

OLIVE OIL

Extra virgin olive oil has always been a precious commodity throughout the Mediterranean, and for this reason the most widespread superstition about it is that accidentally spilling it brings bad luck. The antidote is to sprinkle the spilled oil with salt while moving your hand in the shape of a cross. It is used as a magical remedy in many rituals, from treating styes to warding off the evil eye. The shape of oil drops in water indicates the type of curse: if they spread until they become transparent, it means that the spell is working and is particularly powerful; if the drops join together, there are two people to beware of; if they come together in a single spot, it means that it is a person close to you or even within the family who has cast the spell (*affascino* in Calabria). As well as being an essential part of Italian cuisine, this product is also part of the ritual tradition and is used in many preparations, such as medicinal ointments and cosmetics.

(+)

BAY LEAVES

*L*aurus nobilis has been used in magical rituals since the time of the Latins, and its symbolism, associated with victory, beauty, and poetry, still makes it a key ingredient in a wide variety of preparations. It is also used to flavor meats and soups, while medicinally it is used to make decoctions that aid digestion. In the Middle Ages, in Valcamonica (northern Italy), there is evidence of the use of bay laurel by women accused of witchcraft, who tied a twig to a string to aid in divination. Bay has also been used in many preparations, ointments, and ritual tools of folk healers, some of whose recipes have survived to the present day. A practice dating back to Roman times, and continued in the countryside until a few decades ago, was to burn bay leaves to predict future harvests: a lively crackling meant abundant fruit. A sprig of laurel hanging in the house wards off negative energy, while its leaves can be chopped up and placed in small bags as amulets to attract good luck and success.

(+)

MINT

Mint is a medicinal plant with a soothing effect, used in syrups and herbal teas for coughs and sore throats. As well as clearing the respiratory tract, it has purifying and invigorating properties and is also used in mouthwash and hair conditioner. Capable of growing in the humblest of places, it is a symbol of sobriety and, in the case of peppermint, also of virtue and wisdom. But the plant itself is also associated with Recate, the mistress of all witches and magical creatures, and it is for this reason that it often appears in magic potions and infusions (it is one of the "St. John's herbs"). In Italy, mint was considered a remedy to protect children from curses and diseases. In the South, it was used in places where they cured tarantism, a form of magical possession that was treated with ritual songs and dances. Also considered a stimulant for passionate love, in Salento (Apulia), it was prepared as an aphrodisiac infusion. Planting it in one's garden brings wealth, while finding it in bloom on a midsummer's day brings eternal happiness.

(+)

ROSEMARY

The evocative name of this hardy plant (a symbol of memory, strength, courage, and protection), which is widely used in traditional Italian dishes such as meat, comes from the Latin *ros marinus*, which means "dew of the sea." In ancient times, it was dedicated to Aphrodite, the goddess of love, so much so that it was used to decorate wedding banquets, and it was widely believed that those who touched a flowering bush would soon fall in love, while those who could not smell its scent were incapable of true love and therefore unworthy of it. Obviously, this deep connection to the realm of Eros made it perfect for love potions, aphrodisiacs, and rituals related to fidelity and fertility. Popular tradition also says that putting a sprig of rosemary under your pillow will promote prophetic dreams. In the love language of flowers, it means a happy heart: giving it as a gift is the same as saying, "I'm happy when I see you," making it a message of affection and love.

(✦)

ARTEMISIA

rtemisia includes several botanical species: the most used, also in phytotherapeutic preparations for its antibacterial and fever-reducing properties, is sweet wormwood, but there are also *genepì* and tarragon, among others. All species are used in cooking, herbal medicine, and liqueurs, but one of its most intriguing characteristics is its reputation as a magic herb. The ancient Romans, for example, wore wreaths of it to ward off bad luck. According to Christian legend, it grew in the Garden of Eden in the path of the serpent to prevent it from reaching Adam and Eve. For this reason, it is still believed to ward off evil forces. It is also believed to protect travelers. In Italy, it became known as a pilgrim's herb, and it was customary to put a few leaves in one's shoes before setting out on a journey as protection against dangerous animals and negative forces.

(+)

ST. JOHN'S WORT

St. John's wort is one of the greatest magical plants, with numerous beneficial properties including as an antidepressant, sedative, and antiseptic. Since ancient times, it has been associated with the power of the sun. Its genus name (*Hypericum*), translated from Greek, could mean "beyond ghosts," indicating that it is immune to evil apparitions. It is famous for its use on the night of St. John's Day (between June 23 and 24) to prepare the magical water of St. John, which protects against all spells. During the Middle Ages, in Italian popular tradition, the plant was regarded as "devil repellent" and was burned or hung on the door of houses and stables where the devil was believed to be hiding. It was also used as an amulet to carry in one's pocket or on one's clothes to protect from demons. Even today, infusions, creams, and oleolites (St. John's wort oil is used in healing burns) are prepared from the flower of the plant, not only on June 24, but also on sunny Sundays between May and August.

(+)

TOBACCO

Tobacco arrived in Italy from Lisbon in the second half of the 16th century, thanks to Cardinal Prospero Santacroce. After receiving the seeds from the Pope, he distributed them to various religious orders, who began to cultivate them in monastery gardens, convinced of the medicinal properties of what was then called the "Holy Herb." The monks then distributed the seeds of the plant to peasants — although with different times and in different ways in each region — and by the 17th century, the cultivation of the so-called "Prior's Herb" had spread throughout Italy, where it is still cultivated more than four centuries later. Although the harmful effects of tobacco smoke on health are well known, this plant is still one of the most cultivated in the world and is used in other sectors, especially in agriculture, where it is used as a natural insecticide. In the South, when preparing the deceased, it was customary to place a small amount of tobacco in the coffin, to emphasize its importance in rural life and as a comfort for one's journey to death.

(+)

WHEAT

An indispensable element, present on tables all over the world in various forms and recipes, wheat has beneficial qualities and numerous organoleptic characteristics. It has been the cornerstone of rural life for centuries. There are many traditions linked to this cereal, including the Passion of the Wheat in Lucania (Basilicata), a choral rite that symbolically staged the overcoming of winter and the subversion of social roles. During Easter, *sepolcri* (graves) are prepared, in which wheat is germinated in balls of cotton. The tradition is still alive in Calabria and symbolizes the rebirth of Jesus. The grains must be planted about 20 days before Holy Wednesday, and when the sprouts appear, they are decorated with flowers and colored eggs and taken to the parish. The pale wheat grown in the white cotton represents the body of Jesus in the tomb, which is born again on Easter Day, a green and vigorous sprout, symbolizing the power of rebirth.

(+)

HELICHRYSUM

I ts name derives from the Greek words for "sun" and "gold," and its silvery leaves, together with its extraordinary resistance to decaying, have made it one of the most magical herbs since ancient times. The Romans decorated tombs and sacred places with its flowers, while in rural Italy, from the Middle Ages to more recently, people let it dry where they hung their clothes and handkerchiefs to infuse them with its soothing powers. It is good for coughs and has anti-inflammatory properties, which makes it, when transformed into an oleolite, a perfect remedy for skin diseases such as dermatitis and eczema. A Sardinian tradition links this flower to the possibility of discovering one's marital destiny. On the eve of St. John's Day, young girls would tie a colored ribbon to a helichrysum plant, and the next morning they would check which insect had landed on the flower to try to predict their future husband. For example, a fly would have meant an idle husband, while an ant would have meant a hardworking one. If nothing landed on the flower, the ritual would be repeated the following year.

(+)

LAVENDER

This aromatic plant has a series of magical, esoteric, symbolic, and soothing properties that give it contrasting meanings. Since the time of the ancient Romans, it was associated with the cult of Venus, the goddess of love, and was therefore celebrated as a symbol of fertility and purity. For this reason, it was one of the most popular ingredients for love potions and aphrodisiacs, a custom that has been preserved today, and is still often found in bridal trousseaus, in bouquets, and as a gift for brides. In the Middle Ages, Italian folk tradition attributed to it the power to cure snake bites, and at the same time it was commonly believed that these animals made their nests in its bushes. This is another symbolic value of the plant, that of representing mistrust. Contemporary phytotherapy recognizes the calming and pain-relieving properties of its essential oil; it can be used in the form of an herbal tea to treat insomnia and respiratory problems, while its oil heals wounds and can keep insects away.

(+)

WINE

Wine is one of the most beloved parts of the Italian culinary tradition, and for this reason it carries with it a series of beliefs, rituals, and superstitions. Throughout the peninsula, the custom of toasting happy moments with sparkling white wine is linked to the characteristic sound of the cork, a small pop that is believed to ward off evil, scare away spirits, and bring good luck. From ancient Rome comes the belief, still alive today, that it is not good to accept wine from someone who pours it into the glass with the back of the hand down: this gesture symbolizes betrayal, and pouring wine *alla traditora* (that is, "in a manner of betrayal") is still frowned upon at Italian tables. This comes from the practice of Romans who would poison their enemies by pouring poison from a ring with a similar gesture. Another superstitious ritual still in use is to dip one's fingers in accidentally spilled wine and touch the back of one's ears for good luck.

(+)

CATIORÀ

The Catiorà grass (*Stachys recta*) has many names in the popular tradition: *siderite*, *cattivorà*, *stregonella*... It is a spike-like plant with small white flowers with purple stripes that, when open, resemble wide mouths. It grows spontaneously in uncultivated fields, in dry soil, on the lower slopes of mountains up to 2,000 meters. In many places, such as the Tuscan Apennines or Lessinia (an alpine group between the provinces of Verona and Trento), the belief in its magical powers is still alive today, as well as its effectiveness in clearing the respiratory tract of winter illnesses. In Lessinia it is customary to collect it "between the two Madonnas," that is, between August 15 (Assumption) and September 8 (Nativity). It is dried and then preserved in glass jars. In the Tuscan-Emilian Apennines, a decoction was prepared with which children were washed to drive out fear. It is particularly known as the "herb of fear" because of its use in the popular rite to wash away fears of any kind (fear of an exam, panic, anxiety attacks, etc.).

(+)

DIVINATION

(+)

Certain methods of predicting the future and one's own destiny are common throughout the world, although they take on different forms in different cultures. Many Italian divination rites are linked to Latin ones, which in turn inherited traditions and secrets from ancient Greek culture, which had one of its most prosperous colonies in southern Italy: Magna Graecia, which included Sicily, Apulia, Calabria, Campania, and part of Basilicata. But other civilizations also influenced the composition of prediction rituals that are still practiced in Italy today. For example, the use of tea leaves, native to China and brought to Europe by the English, were added to ancient practices such as reading wine sediments or wax figures, giving rise to the practice of coffee reading. On the other hand, the practice of reading tarot cards is an entirely Italian invention, born during the period of unprecedented creativity that was the Renaissance, and eventually spread throughout the world.

(+)

COFFEE READING

The art of reading coffee grounds became popular in Italy at the end of the 17th century. Ideally, it is done with Turkish coffee, but it is also often tried with Neapolitan or Moka grounds. The reader must be the same person who prepares the coffee, which is then poured into a white cup. After drinking the liquid, turn the cup upside down with your left hand and wait a few minutes before turning it over again with your right hand. When the grounds are dry, you can examine the figures, remembering that what appears at the bottom relates to the inner world, while what you see on the sides relates to the material world. If some of the ground comes out of the cup, the reading is about the past. The reader, preferably practicing at noon, 3 pm, or 12 am, concentrates on the figures left by the grounds, without suggestions, in order to identify symbols and images that can provide answers to the question asked. If the figures are letters, they represent the initial of a person's name or a word relevant to the question; if they are numbers, they refer to periods of time; curved lines mean indecision, a star symbolizes rebirth, a triangle creativity, a square selfishness, a circle diplomacy and fulfilment.

(+)

PALM READING

Reading palms for divination or inspiration is a very ancient practice that is widespread throughout the world. In Italy, over the centuries, it has attracted many enthusiasts and scholars who have written compendia to pass on the art. In the Middle Ages, the philosopher and translator Domenico Gundisalvo combined Arab science and philosophy with classical and Latin ones, officially including palmistry among the divinatory arts. From the 15th century onward, the reference manual of palmistry for subsequent printed publications became that of Andrea Corvo, a mysterious author born in Carpi and considered one of the first scholars of this art in Europe. In addition to the scholarly dissemination of this knowledge, palmistry has always been a popular practice throughout Italy. Palmistry is still practiced and studied today, not so much as a way of predicting the future but as a means of personal exploration of oneself and one's limitations.

(+)

FORTUNE TELLING

R eading cards, and tarot cards in particular, is a widespread practice in Italy, where the oldest decks, originally designed as playing cards, were made. This was in the 15th century, when the first *trionfi* — another name by which tarot cards are known — were made at the Renaissance courts of Ferrara and Mantua. In Ferrara, the Sola Busca was created, a deck with a very dense alchemical symbolism, while in Mantua, the Visconti-Sforza decks were created, which probably gave rise to the classic tarot cards, including the Marseilles deck. The Visconti-Sforza deck has a total of 78 cards, from which other Italian and regional variants developed, such as the Bolognese Tarocchino, the Sicilian Tarot, and the Florentine Minchiate or Germini. Some of these cards can be used to play games (like the Tarocchino), but their main function is as an oracular tool about oneself and the world. These cards are one of the most fascinating methods of knowledge and foresight, rich in ancient iconography, archetypes, and deep ancestral symbols.

(+)

FIRE READING

T he art of reading the evolution of events in fire is a very ancient one, considering that the element itself was part of the origin of human civilization. There is evidence of the spread of this practice in the cradle of Western culture, in ancient Greece and Magna Graecia, or what is now southern Italy. It was here that daphnomancy was practiced, the art of listening to the sounds produced by the hearth. Some bay leaves were thrown into the flames. If they did not burn or make any noise, the answer was bad. The Greeks also practiced capnomancy, the reading of the smoke produced by sacrifices. All pyromantic readings follow a simple rule: a strong fire with little smoke is a positive sign, whereas a weak fire producing a lot of smoke is considered ominous. Interpretations can be based on the intensity of the flame, the number of tongues the fire splits into, the strength of the crackling, and many other details.

(✦)

HYDROMANCY

Hydromancy was practiced in Italy from the time of ancient Rome until the 17th century. The name comes from the Greek *hydromanteía*, meaning "divination by water." The method involved interpreting signs that appeared after throwing objects into certain fountains, sacred waters, or springs that served as places of worship. The Greeks would throw three stones of different shapes (round, square, and triangular) in succession and then interpret the images that could be seen in the circles formed on the surface of the water. Italian witches also used water divination to communicate with the spirit world. Other methods of divination are still used today, such as the floating method, which involves throwing a leaf or piece of paper into a fountain or basin and formulating your question: if the object sinks, the answer will be positive. You can also interpret steam by fogging the surface of a mirror and observing the shapes that form, each of which has a precise meaning.

(+)

TEA READING

Tea reading is a divinatory art that consists of reading tea leaves, preferably black tea, which leaves more defined traces. The tea should be prepared with whole leaves, without filtering. After drinking, a little liquid should be left at the bottom, then the cup should be turned three times clockwise and then upside down on a saucer in order to read the contents left in the cup. There are other factors to consider during the preparation: the steam, which can mean uncertainty, and bubbles, which indicate positivity and wealth. There are four main types of figures that can appear in the reading: people (reflecting feelings, dreams, fears); animals and plants (symbolizing what we can't change); objects (linked to happiness, health, wealth, etc.); and numbers and geometric shapes (which can represent years, anniversaries, presences, or have intrinsic meanings, for example the circle as cyclicality). As with any insight practice, what matters most is the sensitivity of the reader, who will choose the interpretation according to his or her own inspiration.

(+)

WAX READING

This practice of divination has very ancient origins (it is said that coffee divination evolved from wax divination) and has been partially preserved in Italy. It consists of reading the shapes created by the melted wax of a candle, preferably pure beeswax, poured into a brass vessel with cold water. The figures that emerge send messages related to a question previously examined in the burning flame. Candles have always been a symbol of connection with the gods, so much so that they are essential elements in both pagan and Christian rituals. The color and type of flame also have specific meanings that vary from region to region. In southern Italy, white candles represent purity and innocence; red candles, depending on the area, represent passionate love, but also blood, revenge, and war. Green candles symbolize fertility, while black candles are associated with death and mourning. This bridge to the invisible world is not only a link to the magical universe but to the spiritual world in general, and accompanies people in their most important rites of passage, from baptism to death.

(+)

THE *SMORFIA*

The *Smorfia* is an ancient book that associates numbers with the meanings of dreams. It is widespread in various regions, although the most famous is the Neapolitan *Smorfia*, which appeared toward the end of the 17th century. The name seems to derive from Morpheus, the ancient Greek god of sleep. The underlying principle is similar to that of the Kabbalah, namely the idea that there is no sign, word, or presence that does not have a hidden meaning expressed numerically. In the *Smorfia*, this means that every detail of the dream is given a number, which can then be used as game numbers. The dream experience is seen as the bearer of deep meanings that are translated into "good" numbers for the lottery, a state game of chance in which five numbers between 1 and 90 are drawn. After a vivid dream, you have to remember its main elements and look up their meaning in the *Smorfia*, and then try your luck with the corresponding numbers. Among the best known are 48, "dead man speaking," and 77, "women's legs." The *Smorfia* has had a strong influence on Italian culture, art, and cinema.

(＋)

SPIRITS
AND DEITIES

(＋)

One of the most unique characteristics of Italy that sets it apart from other European countries is that within a relatively small territory there is a vast number of different cultures. There is a common thread, but the history of Italy, which has its roots in Greco-Roman civilization (the "cradle of the West"), has been marked by a series of very differing rulers. The result today is that almost every town or village has its own dialect, its own typical dishes, and its own rites and traditions. This diversity is also reflected in the legends, which describe the presence of spirits and local deities and present a series of extremely diverse characters. Almost every mountain peak has its ghosts, just as every spring has its water creatures, every forest has its elves, every village has its house spirits. Magical animals, fairies, gnomes, protective spirits, or destructive devils animate the imaginary and fanciful life of each place, taking their names from local dialects or toponymy. A mixture of fantasy and reality makes up the magical history of the whole country.

(+)

ANGUANE

An ancient figure found in Veneto, Trentino, Friuli, and the upper valleys of Lombardy, these creatures tend to appear in areas with water: fountains, streams, springs. They look like beautiful maidens dressed only in veils, singing melodiously and combing their long blond or red hair in the moonlight. They are kind and benevolent to humans and are said to have taught them how to churn milk to make cheese and butter and are always willing to help women with their laundry. These fairy-like figures are called Anguane. However, when provoked or angered, they turn into *strie* (witches), changing their shape and behavior. They become old and withered, with goat-like legs, and can cast evil spells, kill dogs, empty cellars, and plunder chicken coops. It's possible that they derive from ancient female deities of the woods and waters worshipped by the Celtic populations of northern Italy, symbols of fertility and protectors of fields and livestock.

(+)

MUNACIELLO

The Munaciello (which means "little monk") is a sprite from the folklore of Campania, who is known by other names with similar characteristics in other regions of southern Italy — such as Monachicchio in Lucania or Laurieddhu in Apulia. He appears in houses or haunts mysterious places, such as the underground streets of Naples, which he knows well and where he goes to reach uninhabited buildings or villas he likes. Like his other European cousins, such as leprechauns and elves, he has both positive and negative traits. He can be friendly, hiding coins in the houses he inhabits or playing harmless pranks that can result in lucky lottery numbers, or he can be devious and spiteful, stealing or breaking objects or blowing in the ears of sleeping people. Under no circumstances should you reveal his presence: misfortune will befall anyone who claims to have received a visit. To win his favor, you can offer him food, which he can also turn into gold, but you must not boast of this supernatural gift, otherwise he will disappear.

(✦)

AMMUNTADORE

The Ammuntadore (from the verb *ammuntare*, meaning "to have nightmares") is a mythological nocturnal figure of Sardinian culture. According to some historians, the origin of this spirit dates back to 241 BC, when the island was taken from the Carthaginians by the Romans, but some believe that its origins are even older. Over time, this spirit has been "Christianized" and sometimes takes on the appearance of Satan himself. The Ammuntadore visits people at night, sits on their chest, and brings with it hellish creatures, real nightmares that produce physical symptoms: pressure on the sternum, frightening hallucinations, even death by suffocation. It is a shapeshifter that changes its appearance depending on whom it visits. Once awakened from the torture of sleep, witnesses speak of macabre visions populated by witches, skeletons, and people with bloodied faces. There are formulas and prayers to cast out the demon. To keep it away, the elderly used to place an everyday article of clothing at the foot of their bed.

(+)

COGAS

The Cogas are dark beings of Sardinian tradition, similar to the ancient Sumerian deity Lilith, a female demon who used to kill newborn boys. It is said that, at night, the Cogas enter the houses where a child has just been born to kill it. To protect against this terrible possibility, a reed stick and a blessed rosary are placed near the cradle. It is believed that the Cogas approach the rosary and begin to count its beads, but never reach the end before being chased away by the light of dawn. In the rest of Italy, on the other hand, a broom was used so that the witch would get lost in counting its bristles. In order to confuse the witches, it was also customary not to cut the hair of male children until they were one year old: in this way the witches would have mistaken them for girls and left them unharmed. According to tradition, a Coga would be the seventh daughter in a family of only girls. They are characterized by extreme thinness, a pigtail, and the ability to transform themselves by anointing their joints with a piece of lard melted over a fire.

(+)

LENGHELO

The Lenghelo is a sprite typical of the Castelli Romani (Rome) tradition, which owes its name (which means "elongated") to its tall and lanky figure. There are three variants: the house Lenghelo, the vegetable garden Lenghelo, and the forest Lenghelo. While the first two are simply mischievous, the last is considered evil. The Lenghelo originates from the ancient Roman deities of the Genius Loci and the Penati of the classical era. Although it takes on different names depending on where it appears, the most well-known is the Lengheletto of the Albano Forest, a malicious goblin that deceives people by confusing paths and frightening animals. It is said that you can recognize its presence when, in the middle of the forest, you don't hear any birds flying or singing and you don't encounter any animals. That is when you are near a Lenghelo and you should keep your distance, or else it might set a trap. Apparently it was also a way to keep people away from the woods of the Castelli Romani, which were once infested with brigands ready to rob anyone who ventured there.

(+)

URIA

In Apulia there is the Uria of the house, a protective spirit that defends the economic and physical well-being of its inhabitants. In noble palaces it was represented by a large mask on the archivolt of the front doors or as supports for the balcony slabs, in order to keep away evil forces. In architecture, traces of this invisible presence can still be found today, sometimes represented by the head of a Moor or the head of Medusa. The protection extended to the roof, where the gutters were decorated with grotesque monsters called gargoyles (from the Latin *gargullium*, indicating the gurgling of water). All these guardians of the threshold, who protected the passage between the house and the outside world, are visible representations of invisible forces. The Uria, in particular, discourages quarreling, anger, and swearing, which shows how much it is respected. If someone raises their voice or expresses blasphemous words, they remember that the Uria "takes it badly" and might leave the house, depriving it of its precious protection.

(+)

BORDA

In the Po Valley (which crosses several regions of northern Italy), there is a figure called the Borda in the Modena area, but also known by various other names, such as Bordana in the Reggio Emilia area and Bordoeu in Milan, which means *orco* (ogre). This creature has frightening characteristics: described as a kind of witch with a horrible appearance, she wanders blindfolded on foggy days through the marshes where she lives, killing anyone she meets, especially children. The personification of the fears associated with the marshes, her origin seems to be rooted in Celtic rites linked to water spirits called Borvo and Bormana, who presided over thermal springs. Many place names related to water, such as the river Bormida or the spa town of Bormio, derive from the name of these creatures, which also gave rise to the French equivalents of the words "fog" and "mud." In several Romagna lullabies, the Borda is invoked as a threat, with its noose ready to strangle children who don't want to sleep.

(+)

FOGLIONCO

The Foglionco (or Foionco) is present both in the Garf-
agnana (hilly area in the province of Lucca) and in the
Emilian Apennines between the Secchia and Panaro
rivers. The name refers to both a real animal (it's not clear
whether it's a pine marten, a stone marten, or a skunk), but
above all to a mythological creature with disturbing characteristics and supernatural abilities. It is a nocturnal creature
that abhors sunlight, has three legs, can fly (though only for
short flights, similar to those of a chicken), and feeds only on
blood. It has yellow eyes that glow in the dark, and while it
doesn't seem to attack humans, preferring smaller prey, it
does slaughter animals in a vampire-like manner, making it a
disturbing and feared predator. It is said to be very lazy, to the
point of mating only during earthquakes, taking advantage
of the movement, and to have a taste for Lambrusco wine. In
some areas, such as Viareggio, it apparently can also transform itself into a flying snake.

(+)

SERPENTE REGOLO

Serpente Regolo comes from the traditions of various regions of central Italy, from Tuscany to Lazio, and has its roots in legends about the basilisk, or "king of snakes," to which its name, meaning "little king," refers. Common snakes and vipers can turn into Regolo in various ways: if they live for more than a hundred years, if they lose their tail, or if their head separates from their body. As Regolo, they have the evil power to immobilize their prey with their gaze and then devour them. They usually live in the undergrowth, near mountain gorges or in stony riverbeds, and they can take different forms: normal snakes, but of extraordinary size (wide body and large head, like that of a newborn baby), or they can have legs, be winged, have two heads, or appear conjoined. Their presence is announced in various ways, such as a terrible stench that confuses their prey, or muggy weather that causes illness.

(+)

CIALARERE

The Cialarere, also known as "Brides of the Wind" or "Creatures of the Wind," are magical figures from Lombardy, found throughout the Italian-Swiss border area, particularly in the province of Sondrio and the canton of Ticino. According to some beliefs, these spirits appear as elves, while others believe they are beautiful maidens dressed in green who fly through the air four times a year, creating dangerous whirlwinds. They swarm from one valley to another, flying so fast that they move the air and magically sweep away some animals, as well as frightening the cattle and causing them to run wild. They are generally described as mischievous but not malicious creatures: in fact, they always allow the cattle to be found. In some villages, however, they are described as witches who kidnap children from unattended cribs. To prevent this from happening, people would place the babies on hay or sprinkle breadcrumbs on the ground to distract the Cialarere, who would stop to count them.

(+)

HISTORICAL
FIGURES

(+)

T hroughout Italy's thousands of years of history, in addition to the most famous historical figures that we
study in textbooks, there have been others who have
often been relegated to the background or who are known
mainly through esoteric traditions. These are men and wom-
en whose role in society straddled the boundary between the
ordinary and the supernatural world, such as healers who prepared potions to cure panic attacks or children born wrapped
in their amniotic sac (called *nati con la camicia* or "born with
a shirt"), who were believed to have magical powers useful to
the peasant community. There were people labeled "witches"
or "sorcerers" who were subjected to historically document-
ed trials and who became legends beyond their time and the
places where they lived and worked. The study of these figures
allows us to rediscover the beliefs and the evocative telluric
energy that allowed a deeper connection with nature and the
secrets of the world, and to satisfy our curiosity about often
neglected aspects of history.

(+)

JANARE

A Janara, also known as the "Witch of Benevento," is a figure of legend and reality, rooted in the region of Irpinia (Campania). The Janare were actually healers, experts in herbs and medicinal preparations, who helped families with traditional remedies. Over time, their role in society was weakened and they were increasingly marginalized to the point of being associated with witches and suspected of practicing dark magic. It is said that the witches of Benevento used to gather under a large walnut tree on the banks of the river Sabato. This legend probably originated around the middle of the sixth century AD during the invasion of the Longobards, a pagan people who practiced tree worship and who, according to some scholars, influenced those who had not yet converted to Christianity. At that time, the goddesses Isis, Hecate, and Diana were still worshipped, and the name Janara may have come from Dianara, or followers of the Roman goddess of the moon. Another hypothesis is that it comes from *Ianua*, which in Latin means "door," because to protect the house from the Janara, an upside-down broom or a sack of coarse salt was placed by the door. The idea was that a witch would count the pieces until dawn, when the light would drive her away. In the 19th century, a pregnant Janara was burnt at the stake because she was said to cast spells and curses.

(+)

MADGÒN

A Madgòn (or *medicone*, meaning "great doctor," also used in its female form, Madgòna) is an important figure in the tradition of the province of Piacenza, Emilia-Romagna. This role was assigned by an elder, usually a relative, and generally to a *settimino*, a child born in the seventh month. They had healing powers based on a combination of magic, religion, and esotericism. They could cure many ailments, including muscle strains, sprains, and mumps. For example, to treat whooping cough, the patient had to be taken to the Po river with some elder twigs in hand; then the Madgòn would find some roots in the ground and bury a hard-boiled egg, brought by the patient, next to them. It was believed that the plant would absorb the cough and free the patient. Olive leaves and coins were used to treat rashes and severe headaches. As with all practices associated with rural tradition, the Madgòn never asked for money, but accepted gifts in kind, such as fresh eggs or bottles of homemade wine.

(✦)

GENTILE BUDRIOLI

This extraordinary woman, who lived in Bologna in the 15th century, was also known as *strega enormissima* (really great witch) because of her skills as an herbalist, healer, and astrologer. She cultivated her love of science by attending astrology classes and became an expert in herbal medicine under the guidance of some Franciscan monks. One of her most illustrious patients was the noblewoman Ginevra Sforza, who called her to Mantua to cure her daughter Laura, the wife of Giovanni Gonzaga. Despite the highly regarded skills that made her famous among the most influential families and allowed her to climb the social ladder (or perhaps because of it), she was accused of being an "evil" witch who caused the very illnesses she then cured. Arrested and tried by the Dominican Inquisition, she was sentenced to be burned at the stake for bewitching and causing the deaths of many people, and for being in the service of the Devil. She was burnt alive in Bologna, in the central Piazza San Domenico, in front of her house. Her ashes were scattered to the winds without being buried.

(+)

BENANDANTI

The Benandanti, or "good walkers," are typical figures of Friuli, belonging to a pagan-shamanic peasant cult based on fertility that was widespread between the 16th and 17th centuries. This rural cult was characterized by small communities whose members had a specific characteristic: they were all born wrapped in amniotic fluid, commonly known as *nascere con la camicia*, or "born with a shirt." Part of the amniotic sac was kept by the mothers, blessed and kept as an amulet in a small bag that hung around the neck of the chosen one. The Benandanti were believed to be able to take on different forms, from small animals to puffs of smoke, to join their companions in fighting witches and sorcerers and to bring prosperity and abundance. Like healers and medicine women, they were at the service of the community's health and could also free people from the evil eye and spells. They could also see the dead in procession and hear their messages. From 1575 they were declared heretics by the Holy Inquisition.

(+)

MASCIARE

T here are many names for those who, according to popular tradition, have magical powers, especially in southern Italy: Magara in Sicily and Maciara in Lombardy. The term comes from the late Latin term *magia*, meaning "craft" and is also the origin of *megera* (evil witch). The term was so widespread that it also became a surname, such as Masciari or Masciaro, especially in the province of Catanzaro (Calabria). The Masciare have been the subject of many studies, particularly in medical anthropology and psychiatry, which have investigated their role in the treatment of various diseases, from syphilis to male impotence, and the function of magic formulas and recipes in their magical practices. These special healers were often consulted until the 1960s, especially in Basilicata, and even today people turn to them to ward off the evil eye and to soothe heartbreak.

(+)

ACCABADORA

This term could derive from the Sardinian word *s'ac-cabbu*, which means "the end," or from the Spanish *acabar*, which means "to finish." It refers to the women charged with bringing death in the popular tradition of Sardinia. Stories about them have been handed down almost in the form of legend, since a taboo has obscured the historical aspect of their existence, due to the veto (conditioned above all by religious dictates) on euthanasia. The Accabadora were called upon in cases of illness so serious as to make life unbearable, in order to end a painful existence in a compassionate and ritual manner, with a blow inflicted by an olive branch or a very large wooden hammer, examples of which can be found in some ethnographic museums, such as the one in Luras. Another practice involved removing all sacred images and objects dear to the sick person from the room, in order to make the detachment of the spirit from the body less painful. The Accabadora could be contacted by the sick person himself or by his family members, and did not have to receive any compensation, because "giving death" could not be paid for, according to religious precepts.

(+)

MATTEUCCIA DA TODI

The full name of this woman, who lived in Umbria in the 15th century, was Matteuccia di Francesco di Ripabianca, also known as the Witch of Ripabianca, after the village where she lived. She is remembered as one of the first women accused of witchcraft, and after a trial held in Todi in which she confessed under torture, she was burned at the stake. The charges ranged from having performed magical healing rites to having traded in love potions, and even included more brutal crimes such as infanticide. Matteuccia is defined as an *incantatrix* as she was a healer who could use numerous spells and ritual gestures. The acts of her trial, written in Latin on parchment, are preserved in the Municipal Archives of Todi and have allowed us to trace a formula that the woman declared she used to levitate: *Unguento unguento, mandame a la noce de Benivento, supra agua et supra vento et supra at omne maltempo* (ointment, ointment, send me to the walnut tree of Benevento [a tree consecrated to the god Odin] above the water and above the wind and above all bad weather).

AZZURRA
D'AGOSTINO

(+)

Azzurra D'Agostino is an author and anthropologist who is interested in tarot cards and tarot reading. She still lives in the small village in the Tosco-Emilian Apennines where she was born. She has published various poetry collections, for which she has received prizes, and writes for the theater, for both young and adult audiences. She has published children's and young adult books. She wrote the *Oracle of Destiny* deck and the book *Dreams & Symbols: 300 Simple Ways to Decode Your Dreams*.

ELISA MACELLARI

(+)

Elisa Macellari is an Italian-Thai illustrator and comic artist born and raised in Perugia and now based in Vigevano. Since 2012, she has worked for national and international publishers and magazines. She has published three graphic novels that have been translated in seven countries. In 2024, she won the Gold Medal for Autori di Immagini in the comic book category and received a special mention at the Bologna Ragazzi Awards. She also illustrated *Novice Witches and Apprentice Wizards: An Essential Handbook of Magic*.